AF261298

THE LONGEST WAY UP,
THE SHORTEST WAY DOWN

Eric Raymond Ducksbury
AMPC/RPC/Northern Command No:
13074483
242 Company Section 4, CPL Ducksbury

Foreword by Fiona Murphy

Foreword by Fiona Murphy.

A first and this second reprinted paperback edition published
worldwide in 2024 by Swale Haven Publishing

A catalogue record for this book is available from the British
Library
ISBN 978-1-3999-9598-6

In loving memory of
Eric Raymond Ducksbury
1919-2012

Contents

Pictures

An Old Soldier Remembers
Foreword by Fiona Murphy

Following Remembrance Day each year, one old soldier remembers something quite different; his *joining* the Army.

Eric Ducksbury (92) of Tuxford, Newark, reflects on the day, 28th November 1940, when he waited at Doncaster station to board the train to Bradford, beginning his Army Service.

With memories still vivid and clear, Eric often tells his family of the war years. As a Nurseryman, when he was posted into The Auxiliary Military Pioneer Corps (AMPC), Eric found himself comfortable working the land and growing the food that sustained Britain during the war years.

After call up, in 1940, Eric had to undertake the full military training. He was pleased when he found he was to be issued with a tractor, rather than a rifle. He grew crops for the units training and stationed in the North of England and to feed Italian Prisoners of War held locally.

He had Land Army Girls and German Prisoners to support him.

Demobbed in 1948, Eric went into farming. This was a natural next step for him and his family. He also has fond memories of the type of tractor he used in wartime years, the Fordson N. Later, Eric became a collector of the tractor type and the Ducksbury sons have followed suit.

In the summer of 2011, Eric visited The 40s weekend at Rufford Abbey. This rekindled thoughts of the wartime, and his family found him a WW2 tunic, which he now treasures.

Bearing the sleeve badges of Northern Command and the shoulder tapes of the AMPC, Eric found out his Army Service book to keep with it.

"I am having my memories written in a book," Eric says. "It will be called 'The longest way up, shortest way down.' As any serving person knows, that is how the salute is taught."

The AMPC, part of Britain's Expeditionary Force, was renamed The Royal Pioneer Corps by King George VI, following the D-Day evacuations.

A poem based on The Farmer's Toast
/ God Speed the Plough, circa 1603

> *Let the wealthy and great*
> *Roll in splendour and state.*
> *I envy them not I declare it.*
> *I grow my own wheat,*
> *I bake my own bread*
> *I weave my own cloth and I wear it.*
> *I eat my own lamb,*
> *My own chickens and ham.*
> *I shear my own fleece and I wear it.*
> *I have lawns, I have bowers,*
> *I have fruit, I have flowers.*
> *The lark is my morning alarmer*
> *So my jolly boys now*
> *Here's God speed the plough*
> *Long life and success to the Farmer*

A favourite of Eric's.

Chapter One: The Beginning
(of the book, and of my life)

Today is my 92nd birthday, 1st October 2011. This is my story about this very day seventy-four years ago, the events that preceded this and those that followed.

I was born to Gordon Hedley Ducksbury and Christina Margaret Ducksbury (nee Barlow of Barlow's Bookmakers and Binders, West Hartlepool) on 1st October 1919; a result perhaps of some post First World War revelry!

We lived in the County Hotel, Lancaster until the death of my paternal Grandfather. It then became apparent that the Railway Company would no longer continue the tenancy to my Father or his brother Harry. However, my Grandfather had left two-thousand pounds each, a lot of money in those days, to both his sons. Uncle Harry took his and my Grandmother and stayed at the George Hotel in Huddersfield.

My Father used his money to buy the Ram Hotel at

Newark. I was two years old when we moved there. At that time, it was a pub; coaches and horses would drive in the front and all the stabling was at the back. I remember it all.

1: Eric and his sister Beryl visiting The Ram in 2006 (The Newark Advertiser)

My Father was one for something better all the time and he would go frequently to London with my Mother and me. We would stay at some of the best hotels like the Imperial. All the time he was looking to see how they were decorated, what the lavatories were like, how the service was – and then he would come back to the Ram and replicate ideas there. This is how the Ram became a fine hotel.

I spent much of my time in the kitchen with the kitchen hands and porters. They taught me about mushrooms and how to ferret. I even managed to acquire a pair of hob-nailed boots. I was in my element but my Father was quite unaware.

The hotel business was not at all to my Mother's liking, though. I rather fancy there was trouble between my parents before; but when my sister Beryl arrived Mother declared she would not bring her up at the Ram, so we left and Father went to farm in Fenton.

Farming was not to my Father's liking, but I loved it. There were three-hundred acres which my Father rented from Colonel Royes at the Hall.

Eventually, he packed it in and bought a house on Foundry Avenue in Newark for the family to live in. It is still there. However, in his typical way, he also bought Fourways, a private hotel in Blyth, and ran that himself. It is still a hotel today.

This did not satisfy him, though, and he continued looking for an excuse to do something else. In this pursuit he took me all over the place. He wanted to push me to learn skills that would equip me for 'the finer life', but I still wanted to farm. However, living in the pub, I took to imbibing a few glasses or more of beer and whether my parents knew or not, I will never know.

In 1936, I was sent to Borrowash Nurseries at Derby. My Father paid one hundred pounds for my apprenticeship there. I was close to Elveston Castle, which had fine golden gates; it was a stately home, but I wasn't bothered about that! I was in lodgings, and we used to take the dog out for a walk past it. However I was more interested in seeking out the pubs. I was a pretty good darts player, so I went round different pubs playing darts.

I worked on a market stall in Derby, in the corner, selling cheese sandwiches. The man running it, Bevan, was nicknamed The Baron as he wore knee britches and walked about with a Gladstone bag which he took each night to the boss. One day he became ill and didn't turn up so I took over and took the bag in his place. The boss was quite pleased, and I did this for some time until someone else took over, as several people thought I was too young.

Then the war came.

Chapter Two: Conscription

I stood in Borrowash on 16th November 1940 and watched the bombing of Coventry. I knew I would be conscripted but I was told that if I volunteered, I would get a better job; so I went into Derby, gave my particulars and had the required tests. There was an eyesight test and I didn't see very well in one eye. I had to memorize the card with my good eye, so I could recall the letters which I was supposed to see with the bad eye. This way I passed the test.

I was then asked if I had told my boss that I was volunteering for service, but I hadn't, so they wouldn't take me until I had given two weeks' notice.

During this notice time, my parents fought about what I should do. My Father wanted me to be a Busby Guard but Mother, knowing that like her, I was not the regimental type, was furious. We had a meeting at Fourways Hotel in Blyth; my parents, my boss and I. By this time, I had a job as a cellar man at a pub near my lodgings and I wanted to keep it; so when they asked me,

I said I'd rather not go into the Army unless I had to. Father said I must, though. It was finally decided between them that the National Service form should state I was engaged in agriculture, and was therefore exempt.

All went well for the first three months, but after that, the form had to be completed again. By that time the Baron had died and I was doing the market job, which did not qualify as an exemption, so I was no longer reserved. I was therefore called up.

I recall that day vividly; we had just put hedging on the Borrowash Bypass. My conscription day was the 28th November 1940.

2: Eric in his uniform shortly after conscription

I didn't know where Father was at that time but I went to Mother, and she put me on a train to Bradford, and I joined the Army. It was there that I learned the poem that begins this book.

When I was called up I was in AMPC which became the RMPC after Dunkirk. What happened there is little known. Originally the Auxiliary Military Pioneer Corps were the Soldiers who had vision challenges, lameness, hearing issues or similar and not considered very useful for battle, so were often passed over at such times. At Dunkirk, however, the front-line soldiers needed to get from the boats to the beach, so the AMPC also sailed, and provided assistance. They were not equipped with weapons, but I heard that they knew where some old WW1 weapons had been abandoned, and apparently took them up to give a distraction to the Germans. I heard this enabled the regular soldiers to disembark from the boats. I was not there, but was in the AMPC and I heard about it. When this came to be known the AMPC had its name changed to the Royal MPC.

As it was the AMPC when I joined, I was not equipped with weapons. I was still proud to be a part of the Army and wore my Green Apple on each arm signifying Northern Command as soon as I was able to get hold of them.

For drill and such like we were taught using a pick axe handle rather than a weapon and I was taught to march with one! I remember one night on guard at the gate with my pickaxe handle; I was even wearing spare Khakis and my own boots, so scarce was kit for the AMPC.

The interesting thing about the AMPC is that the men who were in it were all over thirty, usually they wouldn't have been called up but the Army wanted the WW1 experience that these men had.

Chapter Three: First Posts

At my first post, they were building Nissan huts. This was not to my taste, so I volunteered for everything that came up. At one time they set me on as a staff car driver; but 1 had never driven, so I was sent back. I finished up in a food warehouse at Motherby in 1942, which is still there. My son, Paul, sees it when he goes on tractor runs nowadays. In fact, he went up around 2010 and spoke to the present owner, who confirmed the history. He knew of the old landlord, Jacky, and about the pump that used to be in the corner – and even about the singing they all did for me the night before I left to join a new attachment.

When I was on leave, I went back to Borrowash, and there I met up with a young lady called Monica, to whom I was pleased to offer my attentions! Courting was still the 'done thing' then – although if you were lucky enough to find a few bushes, you could make use of them! Nothing like today though; especially as my young lady was Roman Catholic – it was rather a frustrating time for me!

3: Monica in her Land Girl uniform

My young lady and her sister were land girls, and enjoyed a dance in the local pub. We all had rather a good time, but I couldn't always be there, as I had to go wherever I was required by the Army. One day, Fred Barber, the bloke who kept house where we all lodged, wrote to me. I was handed the letter by the postman in York when I was stationed at Mickelby. I was standing on the Ouse Bridge at the time. It said, "You'd better get over and sort these two out, as they are out of hand, mucking about with the local pub people at the Shilling Hop pub." He said my young lady was going off with a Sailor on Saturday night – he thought to the Wilmot, but he didn't know for sure.

I decided right away to head over and sort the Sailor out. I was very cross indeed, and I don't often get cross. I was very upset to hear that he may be 'carrying on' with my young lady. By Saturday dinner time, I was outside of York; and though there was not much traffic then, there were a number of Army vehicles, so I could still hitch. I thumbed it to Derby, then took the bus to Borrowash. When I arrived, he had gone and has never been seen or heard of by anyone since. Perhaps someone had warned him. I'll never know, but I was quite happy to return to my young lady again; I very much enjoyed the visits to the nursery greenhouses and our private walks – until we met Fred while he was out shooting rabbits! I found myself learning to rabbit and go ferreting after that.

Chapter Four: Monica

I was pretty sweet on Monica, but my Mother wasn't keen at all. It upset me that my Mother didn't want the marriage and I didn't know who to ask for help in this. I was attached at the time, rather than with a specific troop, so nobody really knew me well.

Around that time, I was planting at the convalescent garden for Army recruits. There was a Sister there, an Officer in the Women's Royal Medical Core, who invited me in for tea occasionally. One day, there was a storm, so she asked me in. I remember sitting in the kitchen at a huge table, which was built around a real tree that grew in the centre and formed a chopping board! For some reason I mentioned the problem with my Mother's opinion to the Sister, and she asked me, "Do you love this girl?". I replied, "Well, yes, I think so." She then told me not to listen to anything that anyone else said; so I paid no more attention to my Mother's opinion and got married. It meant a lot to me, that the Sister listened to me and saw things from my point of view.

In April 1945 I got married at the Church in Harrow-on-the-Hill, London. We married there because that was where my wife lived at the time. Her sister had lost her husband, who was shot at Monte Casino, and she was understandably having difficulty coping with it all, so Monica went to look after her.

I decided to become a Catholic prior to my wedding because Monica's family were all practicing Catholics. I was taught by the priests and used to turn up for lessons on my tractor.

On the day of my wedding, I had to get all my Army uniform on, including my hob-nailed boots, and I set off to walk over the bridge at Harrow. On the way, I saw a bloke struggling with a wheelbarrow full of bread, so I helped him on my way to Church to get married! I don't expect there's many who go to their wedding in that way now. The girls were in Land Army uniform but had flowers in their hair.

After we were married, we went to an hotel near Weymouth for honeymoon, and made up for lost time! Eventually we decided to take a walk and I remember noticing there were static water tanks everywhere.

We began married life in Weymouth, initially staying with relatives; but eventually we made our way back to Newark. We borrowed a car from Mac Rhodes' Uncle - I recall it was the same car that rescued him when he was knocked down by horses. I drove it, but I had no licence. We stayed one night at Gunthorpe as I had some leave.

I always consider it remarkable that I was never sent abroad, but was 'reserved'. The troop before mine, 241, went to Iceland; but 242 never served abroad. Perhaps it was all to do with my Guardian Angel!

We had seven children after we were married, and if it hadn't been for the early morning milk van calling, we might have had as many as in a football team! Two of my children, Mark and Anne, now live in my village and they visit often.

I don't know how I would have got through some parts of my life without my Catholic faith. In particular, it helped me when I lost two of my children within weeks of each other: my son, Michael, whose tractor remained at my farm; and my daughter, Clare, who has an empty grave next to his in Retford Cemetery, because she lived in Canada.

Chapter Five: Army Stories

Whilst I was attached to the Royal Artillery in Chapeltown, I woke up one morning and saw the hut was empty. All the beds had been slept in and just left. I made my bed and went to get breakfast, but no-one was there – not even in the cookhouse or outside by the lorries. I was the only person on the gun site there. I didn't understand it. I looked everywhere; papers were all over the place in the office. Then I saw the gates were wide open and one or two civilians had drifted in on the scrounge. A few of the older men came up to me and I said I was alone. One of them said, "Well, it's D-Day, they've all gone to the coast in a convoy from Sheffield." I waited for them to return but no-one did. My Officer knew that I had remained at the camp, though, so he got me attached to the Auxiliary Territorial Service girls so I could be fed at their Mess. I was told to go there and sit in the dining room, and that they would give me a meal, and they did. I didn't sleep there, I slept at the barracks and worked there; I just ate with the girls.

***

Another time we had a lot of potatoes to plant at Boughton Camp. This meant putting up the ridges and planting the potatoes in. We were coming from Rotherham and had collected some land girls to help with the job. There was a lad – John Mellors, I think he was called – who used to ride back and forth to eat and sleep but I suggested he stop over at the potato field and eat in the canteen so he could get more work done. He agreed so I put up a shed for him, 8' x 4', by the side of the road. I lent him an hurricane lamp and all seemed to be going well – until one afternoon, a siren went off. Not the air raid alarm, another alarm; and everyone was rushing about worried there was a fire. No fire was found but everyone kept rushing around until someone said they heard that a spy was suspected in the camp. They were looking to catch the intruder; they thought it was a German spy and wanted to know what he was up to.

A jeep pulled up and asked if I had a hut on the camp, I said yes, they asked if someone was sleeping in it so I had to say yes. I was ordered to the office and told I could have been court marshalled for erecting a hut without permission. My Officer Captain Emmaghan had to come and sort it out. I had to apologise and take it down. We had to do potatoes without his help from then on! I never have been one for regulations!

You can still see the site at Boughton, though it

doesn't have gates and railings now.

***

Then there was the Christmas when we had the lorries provided by Shaw & Co. to take the agricultural stuff about. We had a field of wheat to drill on the corner by Boughton then. It was very wet - horrid. We had a horse drawn drill to go behind a tractor. We set off with two or three bags of seed from Brinsworth. There was me, the driver and a Land Army girl to do the job. On the way back to Boughton Camp for lunch we were passing the Old Harrow. It was Christmas Eve and the driver said "Let's go and have our lunch in the pub". So, we left the flat bed lorry in the car park and did just that.

As soon as we were in the door someone said, "Come on Soldier, come and have a drink." We were bought drinks all round, and this kept on all afternoon. We were playing darts and drinking until about 4pm when they needed to close. We daren't say no for fear of offending! When we went outside it was nearly dark, so we didn't bother going back to the potato field – we just went back to camp, which was only around the corner!

We liked the flat bed lorries; in the summer they let the cool breeze in.

***

I wasn't very keen on guard duties and preferred to be stick man - they did lots of varied jobs but it was better than being on guard. They had to wake the girls up!

The Cook had to begin at four-thirty in the morning, so waking the Cook was another job.

Also, as stick man there was always a chance to take forty winks in a shed, or at some venues, in a lorry.

***

It was while I was at Shipley, the Bus Depot, that I was on the gate. There was a wooden raised landing area with a step. It had a double bunk on top and that was where I slept. One night, when I'd had a few, I fell off!

Whenever there was parade, I went, but I preferred to be at the back as I never have been one for the regimental side of things.

Many men wanted to look the part though, and had no idea of how to dress themselves. Their wives had always tied ties and put cufflinks in for them, and they'd never had to lace a boot. I had though, so I helped them. One day, a young chap with aspirations lost his hat, so he took mine; he returned it later and I think he got a promotion!

The men were interested in the Naafi but I didn't reckon a lot to it, so I used to go to the Salvation Army's wooden hut.

There were a few guys at Shipley that didn't last long: one who played the violin; a professional boxer - he never did anything and was always surrounded by his seconds. They were 'reserved' because of their talent so went to teach or be batmen.

One day I happened to be in the Naafi and I saw a guy with a partner; I heard he was a ballet dancer. Sure enough, I saw them dancing in the Naafi; he didn't last long either!

***

We spent a lot of time marching up to Ilkely Moor and then we went to Fulford Barracks at York.

I was put in Jankers whilst there, for going home without leave. I thought I could get away with it, as I knew the schedule and thought I wouldn't be required; but someone wasn't available, so they put me in and then I was found to be absent! I had to parade up and down with my hat off, and I was given fourteen days in the lock-up and had to scrub the floor with a brush.

There were men in the lock-up who were worse off than me, though. They'd probably been there a while. I remember them getting the nib end of a cigarette and using a pin to smoke it. They also cut matches into three or four strips with a razor blade so they could get more than one strike. Desperate times! I was reprieved after two or three days.

***

I was demobbed in 1948, but continued working in the agricultural reserve, managing German Prisoners of War prior to their repatriation.

While there, I was made up to Corporal, and had a civilian man working for me. One day, we drilled a field with oats and grew it for harvesting. When they were due to be cut, I had to get the tractor and sheaf binder organised. We put two new balls of string into the binder box; one man got on and worked it, and one drove. I supervised the other men, who were picking up the sheaves and making them in to stooks; that's how it was done in those days. The binder's tractor was, I think, a Fordson, though it could have been a Fergi; anyway, it kept going all the time and cut all the oats. It never missed tying even one sheaf. It used up all the string and it never stopped, not once. It worked so smoothly I even managed to catch a rabbit during the process!

Chapter Six: A Hospital Stay

In the early 1950s, I was in North Anston, farming. Monica had told me before we were married that she hoped to be a Farmer's wife and live in a big house with children and animals. Whilst I lived there, I got to know a few of the travelling families. One had a baby on the way and I had a lorry; one night the man came and called me to fetch the Doctor. He travelled with me and threw stones at the window to wake the Doctor, who came up to the site near the railway bridge with us. I left them there, but was soon called on again for water and soap. I fetched a five-gallon bucket and a cake of soap and took this to them, and recall being told the baby was born. None of the men went in; they all stood around the fire, so I stood with them. Next thing, a youngster was calling out, "it's raining in." The washing water was dripping through the ceiling, so he was fetched out to stand around the fire with the men.

Some say, now, against Travellers; but I was very grateful to know them because once, they helped save my life.

We had befriended one of the group, Harry Edwards, and he was lodging with us. He would only be so involved as the Travelling people were wary of being too involved with non-travellers. I was ill and being treated for jaundice by the Doctor but I was very badly. When Cliff Rhodes, who I'd done a lot of work with, saw me, he told Edwards to fetch the Doctor quickly.

Edwards went, but the Doctor said I could wait until morning. This incensed Cliff who sent Edwards back and said if the Doctor wouldn't come there and then, he was to go to the police and to say that I had sent him. Well, the Doctor arrived; it was the middle of the night by then, and I was in a terrible state and having to lie against the iron on the edge of the bed railing to relieve the pain. The Doctor said he wanted a second opinion, so I was sent straight to hospital. I didn't know what was wrong at the time but I later found out I had appendicitis. I tried to walk to the ambulance but ended up being stretchered out. The hospital Doctor, Blako Yates examined me and said to get me washed and shaved. I told him if I'd known I was coming I would have shaved first, but that's not the kind of shaving he meant! They operated right away, and when I woke up, I was on a drip in the second bed behind the door. It was an all-male ward then, and they had students to teach on the ward. I remember Blako telling the students what had been done to me and that's how I knew what was wrong.

I enjoyed having a bit of fun with the nurses whilst I was there; I got them to bring me tea when I shouldn't have it, and then we were all in trouble when Matron found the evidence under the bed!

When I was a bit better, I was allowed to walk about the ward and sit by the stove with the other chaps who were recovering. At one point, the man who threshed corn for us came in and we recognised each other!

I watched what went on and noticed that some chaps were having a bit of trouble at visiting time because they needed a bottle to answer the call of nature, but were too embarrassed to ask. I knew this procedure, so I loaded a trolley up when no one was looking and took bottles round before visiting time, collected them up, emptied them in the sluice, and put them back on the trolley. I was in awful trouble with Sister for that!

I did help out a bit though. There was a young chap very resistant to any treatment, and after a bit of a chat I convinced him that as they would treat him anyway, he'd be better off choosing to accept treatment of his own free will. He did and was better in just a few days.

It was a rum place to be as people would die overnight and that was that.

Chapter Seven: Final Reflections

I recall the names of my senior officers, still. Captain Connoraugh and Major Stockton. The Major moved on to be in charge of the whole of the South of England, but still saw fit to keep me working at the camps after a rash of thefts; being a civilian farmer then, he felt that he could trust me, and he could.

***

I worked with Farmer Lockwood at the time, and was friendly with him and his wife. Before he passed away, I called on him – a long time after the war – and his son answered the door. At first, Mr. Lockwood didn't know who I was because I always used to use the back door; but since the house had been changed, I had gone to the front door. I had to remind him who I was by using my nickname, Sam; then we had a long chat.

***

I was very keen on Fordson tractors while in the agricultural reserve, and always remained an enthusiast.

During my working years, I used Fordson tractors, and latterly I bought a Fordson tractor unit with welder, after waiting and saving for seven years.

4: *Eric on a Fordson, his favoured tractor, from the free Farming Gazette newspaper, 1996*

***

I have a jacket with full regalia which I have collected; you never know, it might come in useful if there is a function some time on an anniversary date. The picture here doesn't show the Corporal tapes, but I am trying to sort one out that does. I even have my book, AB64 part 1; and my daughter Hilary found an AMPC poster – there is a copy here. I like reading *The Pioneer* still.

5: Eric, aged 92, in his jacket and regalia

6: AMPC Poster

9 781399 995986